Vint

P\.

abuddhapress@yahoo.com

ISBN: 9798336500110

PW Covington 2024

®™©

Alien Buddha Press 2024

Oxidized

Everything vital
Unspooling from the wheel where I wound
All reason around my blue sky heart and happenstance
Rant, repel, retreat, repeat
Rent and torn, cast to all directions
Like prey, driven over the earthen parapets
That seethe with the patina of treason
Bison and clumbering beasts charge over,
Beyond control and buoyancy, drowned; sunk in dark waters
All assurance eaten at Seder, as we wander mid-Nisan splendor

Swirls of molten hopes eddy from Golgotha to La Guardia
Runaways from every kitchen sink in Tulsa
Special spatial awareness returns in stand-by concourse prayer
Attend to the things blossoming in alloy depths, yet
The tenets of this solar flare remain
Veracity, glassy like ore slag
Howling from the liminal spaces at night
The clocks here have no need for dials or integers or real numbers

Empty copper spools of consequence grow green
Like that queen in New York harbor
Seen from shore

-Winner, The Writer's Garret Common Language Project 2021

Hippo-Colored Hungry

Hippo-colored
Dogmice
Triphop and acid jazz
Afternoon Fresca can
Pickle slices from the jar
Sink and swim
Catalytic slip-stream smoke
Two zips of shake
In the glovebox
Lovebox
Magic fungus time
State lines in the snow
     and
Hippo-colored hungry
Gas station burrito
All's Up
Leather toilet paper and
Cornell '77
On the Bluetooth sound stream
Highway neonspace at noon, occluded

Dogmice
Nickel-plated
Knuckle smash

Nile and Rubicon
State lines in the snow
Hippo-colored hungry

Vampire Conditions

These *are* vampire conditions, Brian
Pulling in all manner of matter and kindness
Taking it all, letting nothing escape
The many varieties of vampire
Stalking through
William Burroughs's Western Lands
Through Milky Way Los Angeles…and worse

Vampirism is as American
As the Internet
Always taking more than giving
Dead and dying, always more than living
Christmas dinner glory carols
Ring
Repeating denial
Re-pealing out
The anti-matter assholes
Of the Yuletide

8 thousand black holes of the soul
So heavy, so dense
Nothing with a name can escape
There's a one-way vampire valve
At the end of this gutter continent

Eventually, we all get out
Born, torn, done, through

Obliterated anew and tossed back in the swim

Alpha Centauri and Pleiades
And all great god-stars crumble in the end
Anything left won't last long on its own
Vampire zone borderline ahead, watch your speed

The emptiness of a blackhole
Coffee cauldron
Neck vein
Drained
So pale
Not even promises
Escape

…like Preacher Casy

Poet

Prophet

Priest like Preacher Casy

Perdition, peace and paradise denied

Dharma from stolen library books in Denver

Oh, my muse

I am heartily sorry

For having neglected thee

Transmissions of visions

On radio at night

Rocky Mountain thunderstorm

Electric

Poet

Prophet

Priest like Preacher Casy

April 20, 2020

I sit and I smoke in my walled, adobe, garden
At dusk
The children have been let out to play
From their quarantine casita next door
School-aged sisters

Their Spanish laughter
In immigrant streets
   under sarape darkness
      en la sombra de Sandia

They giggle
I smoke

And the coming night itself, plays to itself
17 kinds of love songs
   for the stricken
As we each
   in our way
With each passing day
     learn how to forget
        as long as we go on
           breathing

Nero and Caligula

I claw my name into the ridges on the edge of this history
A captive to the testament
Knowing there is no way out
    alive
Goading egoism and Who-I-Am to run out the clock

Falling on the orb that brought it all
Glowing hot pink neon phallus
Beckoning

Sometimes we erect fortresses
Or banks
Or cathedrals
    Hospitals or schools
    Recipes and circumcisions
Some way to leave our mark

Scraping skin from hands
That scratch at glowing crematory walls
Weightlessness and drifting smoke
Does not deliver hope

Yesterday is a foreign nation
A dead language, spoken hundreds of miles distant

From the nearest airport or metro station
Destination in no way guaranteed

Still, we scrawl
On bathroom stalls and border walls
In late Autumn chill
Sculpting history from mysteries

Southern Gothic moonlight misspent
Cuneiform and confusion
Swirl in mad smoke blown
From California wildfires

I am pulled toward the dying light
And with last and fading gasps
I praise Nero and Caligula
Devotions with
No chance of deliverance

Into some lasting, lusty, legend
Stonehard cocks glow
Eternal violet neon sparking

Dirt

Been thinking a lot
About the difference between
Soil and dirt

Dust Bowl winds remove anything
Without chains or money-roots in marble stone
Off, away, to Western Lands
Back to some Cretaceous sea

Sand of the beach
Still isn't soil
But, it can hold water
    and hope
Until enough has died, above, for life
    to stand a chance again

California

Always the continent's lost, last, hope
Cauliflower fields and sand dunes
Sins of all the multitude cultures
Washed and rinsed, out to the sea

Jaguar

The primal cat
Perfected
Riverine
Battling crocodiles
Thick tail
Balancing on tree
Branches
Above the forest floor
Mottled camouflage
Sol y sombra

Predator
And protector
Of all grown back
Reclaiming
Jungle linage

The Blame

3am
In dim and modest
Light
From the console radio
The room spills with low-fi
Steel fan oscillating
Late May

Smoke from a hand-rolled
Kush Indica, medicinal
For sleep

Lit journals, little magazines
Season the floor and furniture
This one from La Crosse,
That one from McAllen
Satanic anthologies
And unapologetic smut

Where does all this wordstainshit come from
Pretending to be poetry
If smoke and radio-waves
Are not to blame?

Kaleidoscope Zodiac

Do the grades and retrogrades
Of Mercury matter?
My windows all replaced by mirrors

Would blood moons
Still bring Apocalypse
Were I to stay inside

Asleep and dreaming
Under tons of concrete ceiling
Hand-held screens

Bring daily astrologers to court
Like preachers on TV
Porn plug-in USB's

So many omens fade from view, unseen
Oracles, unnoticed or avoided
Change the channel, change your mind

Cosmology and astrology
Crumble in the skies of other worlds
Prophesy and mortality, malleable

Point towards the door
Through marble and papyrus
Religious rain and thunder

Family firestorm, seasonal
The stars foretold this flood
The view's never the same from storage

Hold your crystals tight and chant
Namu Myōhō Renge Kyō
Confusing procession and regression

Precision demanded by the
Uncertain and insecure
Trauma cases, clinging to delusion

Gazing skyward for protection
Deliverance distraction inevitable
Genetic attraction

Soothing repetition
Like a heartbeat or a liturgy
I hear your two hands clapping

Mute, unformed, not existing as we see it
Chaos now the greatest fear

Windows replaced by mirrors

Kaleidoscope zodiac keeps shifting
Heaven looks like any other
Walmart Supercenter off the Interstate

And Jesus, just another
Shady, brokedown, hitchhiker
Spare-changing at the exit ramp

Daddy Kink

The first time we fucked
She told me about her Daddy kink
And a lot of other shit, too…
Fucked up shit, man.

But, the more emotionally distant I tried to become,
Like I said before,
None of it was her fault
Or anything she could
Be blamed for, but

The more I came to bed with booze on my breath
Too beat by my job
Beat by the weather
Beat by the world
To give her the pounding
She wanted and deserved

The more she started fucking Steve
The dark-skinned, young
Non-custodial father
That lived in the next building
She started telling me that she
Preferred his cock to mine
Even when I could get it up

Which,
If I'm honest
Was usually only when
I was there
Watching

Watching
As Steve
And whatever other guys
He'd invite over

I'd watch them
In hotel suites
Or our candle-lit living room
Slam themselves
Into Kimmy's
Sweet and liquid
Pussy

Daddy
Yeah- Daddy

I'm pretty fucking sure
She got exactly
What she was hoping
To get
From me

Off Screen

The things we love
Or hate
The most
Prepare us best for death
Unseen, off screen
To just the right or left
Valium nights and
Even the dog needs

Thorazine
Learn to let go
As it gets torn away
A chorus of a million horny angels
Kicked off AM radio
By angry men with
Steel-strong fists
Iron lungs

Inhale
And know
There comes a time
When the air will no longer
Be able
To sustain you

Entertain you

Hitting marks, unseen
Off screen
To just the right
Or left

Saturday

Bacon grease on lingerie
Persian hair, white on black cashmere
It's a rebuilding year
Spectrum split and lit
Saturday is a million miles away

In hiding still, in Omaha
Baking in the sub-strata
The center of America,
Under another assumed name
It's probably never gonna
Get much better

Retrogrades in Michigan
The algorithm knows what you look like
And who you've been
Even in that mask

Sandstone stepping stones absorb the shame
Hiding from the game clock
Falling down in Mountain Time, tonight
Soft machine neon in my brain
With sirens glowing from that high desert airfield

To spoil and waste the perfect
Is true privilege

I'm confused

Dregs and drugs and embers of ambition
Altars, incense, and
Get your palm read by the girl

At craft services
At customs
At the cock tug, come and go, adult downtown theater

Refueling over Roswell
While the desert keeps its mouth closed

Moonlit vapor trails
Slowly dissolve from the sky
With vows made to the departed
Can the end of grief be weighed
Against the cost of memory and mercy?

Are these clinging residues of the dead
And dreams still empty,
All you have to warm you in the rain?

Pain and possibility chosen

Before the silence and conversion of uncertainty

Blankets of tranquility

And night flights to the coast

Prejudice attached

Liberties null, erased

Unkempt guarantees

Splatter on your negligée

    and

Saturday is a million miles away

Rosie's Cafe

The place
Rosie's Cafe
On Madison
With a rose on the sign
Is post-pandemic packed

Folding chairs unfolded
Under folding tables, open
On Saturday
Cowboy hats and trucker caps
Veterans of foreign wars
In stained T-shirts and torn blue jeans
Drink percolated coffee
Bacon, biscuits, gravy
And as
They amble out
To decent Dakota errands and tasks

7th Day Adventists
Sharp suits and business dresses
File in
Filling folding tables
With folded hands
Ordering blanquitos fritos y pan tostado
Hoping to make it to heaven en Español

On a Saturday, Sabado

The timeless, always, Universal waitress
Fills coffee mugs
And splits the check
At every table

As light grey
Late June rain
Falls indifferently
Outside

Greenwood

Freedom

From middle class

Post-war, pre-war

Desolation rows of angels

Brownsville girls

Cody and Johanna

Morning magpie

Singing for that walking-saint

Perfect priest in Mexico

Changing your mind

In that Massachusetts graveyard

I'll find my Walden on the border

Down by the tracks

Always back to the railroad Earth

Always back to Kerouac

In September and October

Always back to the ashes

Range-fire smoke in the air

Ashes of Greenwood

Woody Guthrie sabotage

The machinery of fascism

That tries to snuff the legacy

But that train

That train is still

A coming

Like Jack's last and liquid dream

Building from the ashes

Of Tulsa

Greenwood

Garden Buddha

I enjoy keeping a cheap
Dollar store styrene
Seated Buddha figure
In my front yard flower bed

Where the French hollyhock
Is giving way to Autumn
And where barrio cats
Like to paw and piss
To inter their shit

For roots and shoots
Of future flowers
Dharma wheel spinning
In the Buddhaworld of
Mi 'Burque courtyard garden

Ghost Trees

Cottonwoods bleached
White in the sun
Rio Grande dry sand baking
Spectral and almost glowing
Moonlight mirage with mule deer

Skeletal
Snow melt run dry by April
The ghosts of San Antonio de Rio Bravo

A river killed
By Trinity, perhaps
Downwind
Downrange
Downstream, dry sand blows
Slinking past at midnight
White

Faded
Bleached
Forgotten
As river cedes to desert
Easy hope no longer flows

Chama Street Suite

Mulberry leaves drop
In my adobe courtyard
First frost coming soon

                                      Texas Christmas card
                                      Family armed at yuletide
                                      Safety off season

Snow melt waterfalls
Cold streams meet rivers
Flow to storm warm seas

                                      Power tools building
                                      In immigrant neighborhoods
                                      Realized dream songs

Lucy Luz

Today's college avenue coffee shop precocious
Physics student phenom

Will end up running out the clock a perpetual
Boho underachieving
   underground
   poet
Daughter of Los Alamos

Sharing poems
Once a month
For friends
At an Indian restaurant

Near the marina

Adopting two fat, inside cats
With names lifted from Grateful Dead lyrics

She'll score sleep studies
Under contract
For the government clinic
At Travis Air Force Base
From her El Sobrante apartment
And fuck and foster men

She finds at festivals
And readings

Felons and non-householders,
Wandering monks of Kerouac
Desperadoes of late-Capitalism

That have not yet been born
As she writes her mid-semester paper
On photons and energy waves

The Ways of All Wild Things

Trust the ways
Of all wild things
And animals
The path that lava water takes to sea
Trust the unseen mystery
Phone calls never answered
Letters, never sent
Chances never taken
Dice never thrown
Rivers never waded slowly turn to legend
Mountain tremor nizzle wonder saxophone
Sunset on the Rio Grande, alone
How many million lives have prayed,
   up here
      In vain?

One Day

One day in my nation, 3000 people died
I watched it on TV
With tragic voice-overs and commercial breaks

Young men from small towns signed up as soldiers,
    cocksure and conservative
Eagerly surrendered freedoms
We embraced body-scanning machines and new ID requirements
Show your papers to travel
Trillions were spent on boondoggle technologies
But it made us feel safe

A cop on every corner
Secret prisons in Cuba
Billions of pounds of bombs were dropped
The flag itself was weaponized
And sold at Texas gun shows
No expense nor liberty was spared
All taken by security

Dissent did not exist, from Phoenix to Fort Lauderdale
We started using words like 'Homeland'

Millions killed or maimed since that day, to keep us feeling safe,
When 3000 people died

It kept us proud and productive
Damn, we were proud and strong and wrathful
Because some buildings fell one day

3000 die now *every* day
And most can barely yawn
Is the football game on?

Productivity, still, the idolized ideal
But death's depreciated in value
Divided against ourselves, each inventing our own truth
Rural ignorance and big city loathing
To simply stay at home and do no thing
Too much to ask
Selfishness

Reward centers fed and warped brain chemistry
Where we will never claim to be afraid

3 fucking Thousand, every day
Still, the fetish flag gets waved
And folded over coffins from the chosen wars, on going
Weep for slain soldiers, home from foreign shores

But, fuck today's 3000
Killing is easier to square than compliance
Violence preferred over science

3000 every day, but we want burgers and beer,
    trick or treat and Christmas trees
We want anything but inconvenience, ornamental

And to the overly entertained,
Deaths without explosions
Aren't the same.

Zero Kelvin

Back from the war
I stayed stoned
The next ten years

No desire but to be out
In far solitude
To live lost on the train platform
Airport commuter courthouse
Hospital prison detention
College clinic coffeeshop
Driver license waiting room

Waiting on the sure and unpredictable
Uncertainty
Having long out-wiled the finite
All salvation I will ever need
In a grimy bathroom stall

Southern Gothic crossroads in the night
Stateline rest-stop, drinking
Chalices of inevitable bitter grounds
From brown, paper sacks

The next 10 years

Steady on towards
Zero Kelvin entropy
Nirvana ego-clearance center
Myth and splendor

All must go
All must go

Kung Fu Radio

I find myself again, in need
Of billboards and broadcasts
Broadsides of internet interstate intersectional
America
All that Andy Warhol meta-data
Ironic display of discourse

Communicating these days
Is like watching
Kung Fu movies
On the radio

As snow falls on New Mexico
Shining blankets on adobe mud walls
Melt-water to next spring's
Daffodil and tulip bulbs, beneath

All my digital mirrorwork
Has been draped for Shiva
Tapestries, brought by Chuck Taylor
Like Bodhidharma, from the West
Made east, made Japanese
Insist that no reflection is true
No pixel is perfect

And that even the things
We eagerly throw away
Deserve mourning

Karmic Mountain Sharks

Lessons learned later in life
Like the secret clauses in some Karmic contract,
Coming with kindness,
That compassion be sustained
Maintained

Because lost and feral things need no morality
Because there is no failing in the birds and neighborhood street cats
That I ration out feed and seed for, in condolence

Even when I would rather stay
Sativa stoned
For days at a time
Deep in my peeling self-delusion
Hiding through retrograde daylight

By the ever-swimming power of Karmic mountain sharks
And the sanctity of sheep shit Jesus shepherd
The strays and songbirds
That visit my adobe spot of refuge
Get fed

Every afternoon

Birdshit Satori

Raising my voice and
Waving my arms
Trying to shoo
The wren away
Off her perch
20 feet above me
In the leafbare winter
Mulberry
Because she keeps
Shitting on me
(Who she can't even see)
Standing
Directly below

Instead of simply shifting
Some of my weight
Silently
Over, a foot or two

I stew
Colonial in my frustration
She refuses to fly away at my attentions
My expansionist, occupationist selfset
Beset by nature

And liberation as it manifests

One
White
Drop
At a time

Anti-heroes

As the brutality took hold
It became common virtue
The 60-hour work week
The dangerous, low pay, employment
All the wars and oil rigs

Your eyes never left mine
Sitting in that window seat
Leaving Midland
State police and soldiers at the exits
Below and behind

All the highways
Named for dead soldiers
Dead cops, now
Roads that once inspired songs
And invited wonder
Now draped in flags like coffins
All rise
In surprise
For the TikTok national anthem dance video
Media social, like a disease

But, we had brilliant TV

As the brutality took hold
Anime and antiheroes
Women other women loved to hate
Terror
Shootings at supermarkets and schools
Border walls and ammunition

And, how much longer will it be
Before the patriots come
To reform or remove us?

So, we flee on our own
In red and blue strobes before sunrise
We do it to ourselves
The brutality too skilfully installed
To have noticed as it happened
Every refugee fist
Shaken at the sky, tonight
Demands rain on desert sand
Dry and violent

I taste your desiccated love-salts on my lips
Like jet fumes pressed into powder
The brutality of lust takes hold
Somewhere outside Dayton
When you text from California with your terms

Dry and brutal
Waiting to sift the ashes
Of our pandemic partnership
Fire horizon cruelty and reason

Cruel and edged
Looming large and cold and everywhere
Anti-heroes on TV
Streaming, bleeding, across the orange sky

Your hand is all I see in memory
I'm reaching, retching, stretching
And hanging in the sky

Reluctant Angel

Reluctant angel
She bought those wings with sacrifice
Flesh from her own bone
Through frozen rain and hurricanes
Beauty wings for beauty days
Her world glazed with
Dazzling kinetic balance
Blame the rain and other things
On the way she's always been in motion

The wings were borne of necessity,
    she'll tell you
Every lesson learned
    every feather, earned
But, either she follows angels,
    or they follow her
In this year of everyone's need
This Spring of fever and gasping
    on the border
And, she's there

Charming casita, walking distance from campus
Left vacant in the glowing, turquoise, city
Six seasons

Those wings have something more than
   sanctified you
You have trusted them to keep you safe and fly you home

Trust them still,
                    tonight

The Coffeehouse Near Campus

Un-Capitalized
Principle
Masochistic free-verse at the open mic

Principalities of unreality
Identity
We write our own symphonies
Edit our own obituaries
In dives like these
5 star reviews and acid-jazz synth

The sun is hiding out
Just south; just west, of here
Neon vapor trails and highway flares
Vegas wedding cake
Destitute

Attitude and snowflakes fall acidic
Grow-lights at the hardware store
Digital aftermath of an eight year drought

Peterbilt's and highway piss-stop protocols, observed
Flay yourself tonight in coffeehouse projection
Never better than more of the same

More of the same

Dynamite

Destroy your desires with dynamite
Hold parades for all fallen conscripts
Convicts and Queens of gated community

Bodhidharma carpet-bombed the West
Until all that was left
Were mistrals and mystic misfits
Royal tapestries
Unwoven
Root canals at Christmastime
Be blessed

I've lit 17 fuses, myself, this morning
Shaving mirror after-shocks and tantrums
Trauma center take-out Kung Pao chile
Powder kept dry by force-field of panic
Bile in African sunlight, soaking
Into neon, smoke stained, sandbags stacked behind

Rinzai masters
Sit on carbonated councils
Compounding quarks and nano-bots
Leaving Louisiana on a flatbed trailer
Chained down and rusty, beside the Sabine

Destroy your desires with dynamite
Re-radicalize yourself, again
From within
How much of this dream do you want to believe, anyway?

Flow, Universal
Into the crevices and wrinkles
That time pretends to fill
Winter burns in twilight gleaming flight
Demon decolletage, teasing bankers out on Market Street
Discretion is not called for these days, at all

Burn the ships that brought you here
The documents and currencies you hoard
Saints of circumstance in made-up murder mystery shows
The ebb and flow of failure praised perfection

Each climbs to
Our own orgone-powered tree house

At a quarter past the
Pyrotechnic afterglow

Shining noble

Vortexas

Of course there are good people, there
That's what the soulsuck vortex does
It pulls all kinds from everywhere
The triumphant and discarded
The broken and the thriving
Down the empty, burning, nowherenothing drain

HemoRed gunpowder Christ-fire hate
Where doves decay and flags wave from fortress walls and tombstones

I hear you laughing from Bellefontaine, Burroughs
You called yourself a farmer when you lived there
Tiger nights and lost boys in Reynosa

Crystal shining star of silver hope
Melts in cold reality
Of roper boots and Mossy Oak
Like snow in Spring
And mud in Texas

No state of being to be in

Nykolia

He wrote of the invasion
The way that
A poet's daughter
Writes about suicide

>'The shells are still falling
As I'm cooking breakfast.'

He posted

>'These are the last of the eggs.'

>'I haven't seen my cat in 6 days.'

Then nothing
3 weeks now

And I'm against
Every bomb dropped
Every rifle fired
Every soldier conscripted

And hammered into the
Mechanized machismo of expansion

More so
Any God
That allows artillery
To rain upon nursery schools
And apartment buildings
In Mariupol
In Mogadishu

Mad Swirl

The road is learning how to live
All that road-going

The Blues is learning how to die
Trip taking
Booty shakin'
Forsaken and forgotten
All those melodrama mornings
Total evil rallied up against
Pure love all agape

Careening locomotives
And young women tied to railroad tracks
Fuck that

This is Jack's mad swirl!

Catastrophes called problematic
Solutions hidden, enigmatic
Snap, crackle, pop
And static

The Blues is learning how to die
Sit down

Tune up

Enjoy the ride

Do Not Crush the Fading Ember

Do not crush the fading ember
Orange glowing into ash
Thin smoke stream
Wraps as ribbon
Through the night
Tying ends of the chill together

Do not crush this fading ember
You, who are so huge as to
Do so at will and whim
The fire here warmed you well, through winter

With fuel consumed
And your once catalytic breath removed
The kindness of neglect
Is my only prayer, here

Let the final ash
Turn grey and cold
But slowly

Eternal in the spiral mind inferno

Forgotten

Blood on the Tracks
And Big Sur
Idol glory writer in retreat, ego-wasted
Mid-life exam
Turning your head and coughing

Washing away the once wondrous road
Knowing that the highway took you nowhere
It was only you out there moving
Down to the water, back to the Earth

Back to desolation in New Brunswick
Then to France
Chasing so many childhood carnivals
And movie memories, collected

The sound demands an answer
Shaking hands in the foyer
Back and forth, from Dean to Sal
"Hi. I hear that you're the new me."

Bury us all in unmarked graves
To be forgotten
Like Kaufman

Lodestar

I came into this world
Reserved
Intending to do no thing
To walk in all directions
Everywhere at once
Eyes open
To keep my own gait and pace
Tenderly
Lingering where I should want in the moment
For the day, the year, or longer

I came into this city
Marching
One of legion
Eyes flying, quick to the flame
Where no soft-soled feet could follow
Lightening-passion cocaine sex and trauma
Never quenched

Mountain meadows are not mirages
Reflecting winter whiteglow snow-shine gleam
That light is true as stone, and death and love
And the ocean floor, vaulted to the sky
As tiny and viscous centuries churn past

Snows fall and melt
The mountains barely
Notice

I plan to leave this world
Untidily
My best words yet unpublished
All best loves flashing red
Lodestar true
      and ever shifting

My Brother, Who I Only See at Dead Shows

I only see my brother at Dead shows
He's been out of the hospital now,
Five years…maybe more

We always meet up
Way in the back,
At the top of the bleachers,
Or on the amphitheater lawn

Where few people are
Or where those there are, are altered
Because there's always been something
A little altered
A little awkward
About my brother

And the only place I've
Ever seen him truly happy
Is a Dead show

So, every year
We meet up
Summer or Fall
Sometimes in Boulder

Sometimes at Bethel
Sometimes out by the Bay

And we talk
Of superficial things
And share a jay
Catch up, in our way

As Bob Weir's face
Whiskered as Bobby the White
Beams from the Jumboscreens,
And glows over the pit

My brother's
Easy-dancing tie dye smile
Reminds me…it reminds me…

Morning Glory Wednesday

Her taste and spicy night perfume
Still linger on my face
I leave our restlovingbed

  To the living room and kitchen
  To stoke fire coals
  To reach outside for two
     thin sticks of pine
Kindling
  To spoon ground coffee out
     with pinon, into the filter
  To put Duke Ellington on the music box

It's Wednesday

  …and you have fallen back into sweet sleep for the moment
  To do what I can
  To gild your morning rising
     in the glory, so deserved

Enough To Share

Mountain glowing pink neon at sunset
Night sky fading indigo to stars
Moon orb rising sexual and urgent
From beyond limestone granite
Hardness of all history
Waves and waves of atmospheric lust
Caress her skin and liquid things begin

The chains of fear she left road-side in Texas
Scars she wore for decades, so adorned
Testament to hopes of arriving here, through years
Between the mountain stone and river flow

She's claimed herself
On moonlit nights in Summer esoteric; rare
More than that,
She's found enough to share

Tumor

The Universe
Shrunken
Confined to the size
Of a tumor

And T-cells, taking the role
Of gladiators and giants
Grappling in internal arenas
Within cell walls, in bayou cities

Small-town clinics
With single-mother vocational nurses
Breakfast skipped on infusion days
Silent rides home

Eyes closed
Not even the radio
On

Neither one of us,
Ready, yet
To say, out loud, that

It feels like

The end
Is taking longer

Than we thought it would
To come

Contradiction

Clean Antiseptic
Safe and sterile
Harsh and honest fluorescent lights
On bleach-clean
Stainless steel, secure
Suburbia

Illicit
Smoky sunset, sexy
The romance of uncertainty, rejected
Dreams washed worn and traded in
At risk of liability
Post-post-modern mortem

No one cares about
Honor student run-aways
In these days of consequence
And distraction

Contradicting

December

Sitting naked
I am smoking on my couch
Holding pen

Journal out and open
Counting syllables
Holly on the mantel

My muse, my love
My cockslut postal patron
Cuckoldress
December

Confetti

Diatribes torn from books and movie screens
Scattered before turn-stiles on the floor
Souls sing inside the juggernaut of healing
Completion as the seasons change outside

Half a Camel filter by the dumpster
Wendy's restroom shave and armpit rinse
Napping in the city park as pigeons
Flap and coo and pick up all that's lost

Leaking from too many mid-June weddings
Interviews and immigration lines
Passports made confetti in our image
City shines as mirror-shades are drawn

Dessert

I am eating an American
MRE meal, shelf stable,
Mid-morning and 100 degrees,
Within sight of 4 starving children
In a place where metabolism
Has been weaponized
Where hunger is traded for rage

And they've seen too many
Armed and fatigued, come before me
To believe in even the shadow of hope
Flown in across the sea
    from all the Canaans of Capitalism

Flown in on grey wings of
Cold War champion Nephilim
Survival the only morsel that matters to them, today

And I feel like steaming
Indian Ocean coastwise sewage
The foil sealed rations and calories
I am swallowing, will be valued,
Precisely as shit, by the next sunrise

As famine victims die every hour

I decide not to open the vacuum packed
Brownie snack dessert
Baked somewhere in Northeast San Antonio

There is a Timelessness

There is a timelessness
We'll never touch as mortals
Midnights shared on fire-escapes
      beyond

Communion rail semen-splatter stain
Highway exit coin-delayed arcade
Fluorescent glowing aftermath of Paradise
      be praised

We spend our all, total, lives complete
Waiting in line at traffic lights
In turn-lanes with visors down
      and smoking

Even all our misbehavior
Fears apostasies denied forever
Cathedral floors and catacombs
      laid bare

Wisconsin Cheese at Midnight

Before my winter
Midnight mountain fire
I nibble Wisconsin Cheddar, extra sharp

And all my thoughts of mind turn
To every dairy family, to every cow
To every tractor-trailer driver
Every cheesemaker, grocer, and check-out clerk
Every hope and multiverse of mercy, love, and passion
And I wonder

If they are anything at all
Like me
As I taste the cheese completely
In indulgence

As I hope
They might hope
Their work would be enjoyed

Network Failure

Compass and chart guide true
Yet forsake me at the crossroads
The network is down, this decade of
Autonomous identity
All tangents to be praised

All means and ambition, squandered
Unmade beds in highway rooms, elevated
Holding tight to that magnetized ladder
In hopes of joining the password protected in their privilege
A vein, not an artery; removing the unappreciated

Lost in the mercy of Mercury
There is a trace of heavy metal aftertaste
It turns my belly sour in the pre-dawn
Bounded by the popular demand to dwindle
To make myself silent and unseen in these spaces

Compelling rogues and rebels
To bend as bent and slant
Exactly as expected and directed
I drove here, myself
The entire, unmade, continent behind me

Wear of the road, odometer clicking
Miles and mystery, received as holy sacrament
The network still isn't working for me
Node of redemption shining, unreachable
Steel mesh and razor-wire boundaries abound

Fitting perfectly with the conformity
The hem at the bottom, unfinished and frayed
Network failure
Network failure
Link unfound

Lent

It is the first Saturday
Morning of Lent
I am having King cake for breakfast
Along with left-over Bourbon dregs
And ice-melt water
From a glass stained with bright pink lipstick

Ash stains on my pillowcase with bronzer smeared
Rusty razor tilt a whirl
Sacrifice sanctioned, subjective in these
Late winter, fresh year, daylights
The tiny, hidden, Christ child
Found face down

Clinging to the soggy butt of a Marlboro Light
Fully submerged in a rocks glass

My Neighbor's Grey Cat

Terra cotta glows

In the snow

Outside my kitchen window

Drinking Diet Sprite in the sunlight

Smoking sativa

Blowing smoke

Against the cold window pane

I dream of August

Hiroshima realizations

Settle in about

The clay pots

Half filled

With last year's

Potting soil

In my garden, glowing frozen

Forsaken

By all except

My neighbor's grey cat

And me

Vintage Denim

Fast fashion forward
Now they're trading in vintage denim
All the stock exchanged for art and boxing rings
Echoes out of Louisville
Shotgun with Ron Whitehead
Through neighborhoods and mystery
Riveted and mined up
On the main line

Knees worn through and patched over
All the hues of indigo inside
Dreaming
Stopped and shuddered, laced
Stuttering up stair steps
In long abandoned shopping malls
Sub-urban escalators
Lost in time

They used to remind us
Right there on the plastic case
Be kind
Rewind, seek grace in every face
That passes
Every soiled and stained garment

Tossed into the laundry
Arrives with its own romantic story
Stitched and riveted

Pressed together, pierced, and threatened
Bare, worn faded
Cuffs and hems
Dyed and sewn and covered over

Repackaging the undesired
Into virtue boutique novelty
Immigrant sweatshop
Enslaved cotton fields
Upstream a million years ago

Work clothes become
Recreational adornment
Recycled
Acid washed
Boot cut, button fly

I Live in the House that Jack Built

I live in the house that Jack built
I dine at a moveable feast
Through pastures of plenty on a Northbound train
A toast to 1969 and Flamingo Bar
Raising margarita glasses in Florida desolation

I live in the house that Jack built
I dine at a moveable feast
Accents in French
Or Spanish or hitchhike highway
Schizophrenia-driven Colorado madman
Preaching at a midnight North Beach bus stop

I live in the house that Jack built
I dine at a moveable feast
Mardi Gras mornings with beignets and chicory
Hired onto a Yugoslav freighter to Cork
Fleeing across the water
Staying ahead of gun smoke and seizures

I live in the house that Jack built
I dine at a moveable feast
The town and the city, ever behind me
Before me, a time-warp chimera

Sworn secret in that Salt Lake mirror-room
I am drinking hot drink, all the same

I live in the house that Jack built
I dine at a moveable feast
Discothèque Juarez checkpoint shakedowns
And years in Texas prison camps, be damned
Charleston motel meth market parking lot
Holding out hope for the next time at hand

I live in the house that Jack built
I dine at a moveable feast
In light-rail cars and hotel bars, I've seen them
Married to their misery, heaters set, 451 or more
Discount Southern states and churches
Flying Baptist banners at the courthouse

I live in the house that Jack built
I dine at a moveable feast
Union busted freight car railroad sidings
In Laramie, absconded with the last of last year's consequence
The clock keeps time for no one to take notice of
Retreating to secret libraries of eons

I live in the house that Jack built
I dine at a moveable feast

Catholic seminary run-away student
Circus clown and housewives
Theater ticket counter clerks and nurses
Writing it all down, for later
Later
Later

I live in the house that Jack built
I dine at a moveable feast

Necessary

In your necessary
And pragmatic opposition
To the molten, iron, stars
In my own heart, electric

I also see supremacy
Fields that I could barely plow
Would seldom tend
Never seed

Every passionate grain of counter-balance
Moonlit petals glow
Even in the castles, even in the slums
The solemn and insane combine to sing

In your necessary
And pragmatic opposition
To the power stars that pulse
In my own heart, electric

Beating still
In alabaster hills
Still beating

It's Been a While

I traveled mostly solo, then
Roll into town like desert wind
No rain to give
Backbone and ribs

I'd find a place to sit and rest
Parks and overpasses,
They sheltered me
   (and libraries)
Until I'd have to leave

I hear you've met a working man
Suburban home, insurance plan
And that you've moved
I'm glad for you

But some days in the winter-time
I'll pass by some place, again
Some County Jail or parking lot
Or dive that we slept in
And I smile

But, it's been a while

That Chaves County motel
Where we stole and sold that car
That night up on Mount Lemmon
And Tucson mountain flower
That crazy week in Vegas, and all the words we said
Are they all dead?
(Or) Just in my head?

Sometimes at the break of dawn
I'll wake somewhere again
A truck stop on the Interstate
Or red-lit Lion's Den
And I'll start to smile

But, it's been a while

It's been a while since I looked
And caught my own shadow
The sun's always in front of me
So, that's the way I'll go
And, no, it's not as easy
As it was those years ago
But, I'll still smile

I hope you know

Sometimes in the midnights
Where moon-lit Aspens glow
The smoke and spores of centuries
Are painting kind tableaus
Where the bull elk bugles echo
Down through the ancient Gorge
I'll start to smile

But.
It's been a while

Flushed

It is my own perverse distraction
On these early nights of the year
To dream of a world
Half hallucinated
Where every new noun
Every figment of fantasy
Of horror, hope, or fear
Is quantum-born and nurtured
As far as my distraction and delusion will allow

Then flushed from all existence to the void
Where all decays, then manifests anew, in time

Music in some foreign fractal tongue
Is dancing in my moonlit mind akimbo
A nascent morning climbs across the ridge
Of Watermelon Mountain
Another heliotrope
Another karmic resting place in shining
Shiva and Madonna kiss
In secret, sacred, sunrise
Flushed

Eggshells

I took the wrong train
One time in Dallas
And missed my plane

Ended up riding to San Antonio
With a real estate agent

It was intense and mercurial
And sick and fucked
And transformative

Eggshells up and down I-35

Des Moines 8/23

And what now of this parasite existence?

The technology of plagiarism
Every emulation more toxic than the last
The morning horror

Plastic figurines for sale in gift shops
Magnetized and sanitized
Half as dangerous as yesterday

Twice as armed

Machine gun kindergarten
Play date violence
Charles Whitman Middle School

Draped in vampire resurrection,
So redundant
In the end

A flea, a tick, a scabies crab

On half shell
Jurassic
Astonished by audacity

Sold and served beside the sewer
In the end

Scratch and pick at it

Cordite, pairing well with baptism

Slather it in lotion
In the end
Physics and biology will win

And steer all parasite existence
Onward through this slipstream living realm

In the Air

As a child I'd strain my neck and eyes
After jet and propeller sounds
I'd follow them across my pre-teen imagination past horizons
And yearn to earn
Wings of my own, someday

Ever the arriving vagabond
Yankee air-pirate, barnstormer
I still seek those states and places in-between
Earth and heaven, tease and torment
Chaos and order, descent and ascent

Pilot in command
Stick and rudder, by the seat of my pants
In all my aimless flutter

Only vapor trails to point the way
Hindsight perfect eagle-eyed as aviator
Neither here, nor yet there
Suspended in the firmament
Only ever on the way
In between
In the air…

Airplanes Anymore

The ragged man outside my gate
Doesn't believe in airplanes anymore
The forces of flight, aflame in the night
Or in the way jet engines roar
All allure and mystery, misplaced in a helmet bag
Left on a ready-room floor, last century

Wedding bells and claxons
Toll over Albuquerque Central
Air control hyperbole
He lets eagles and angels
Airliners and jet fighters
Soar into infinity as
So many purple flying monkeys

As he tapes his nylon
Sleeping tent back together
With duct tape in the morning

So ground-bound and down, the sky itself
Can disappear, it seems
Without concern nor warning

High and Holy

In these stolen moments
    we arrange, together
High and holy in our hypocrisy

Subtleties tinged with obscenities
The lies we've relied upon for so long
Winded at the starting line, again

Your morning glowing skin in mountain sun
Intermittently enforced
By lust and love and all other last resorts

Cohorts of the Interstate on-ramp
Like LED's on cardboard
Corrugated tin bent into a track-side shanty in Chihuahua

As the ghost of Pancho Villa lingers between
The train station and the prison

In these passing hours, shared
Pilfered from the people we'll become
So separate

Ordering a la carte in genuflecting tones

Before the judgment throne
Paint your lips, kneel here,
Let us pray

Fully engorged and fleshy
High and holy in our hypocrisy

PW Covington has been recognized as the 'Beat Poet Laureate of New Mexico' (2024-2026) by the New Beat Poetry Foundation.

For over three decades, Covington has criss-crossed the continent sharing poetry and energizing audiences with his full-tilt presentation style and street-earned subject matter.. He has been invited to perform from the Havana International Poetry Festival in Cuba to The Beat Museum in San Francisco.

A multiple Pushcart and Best of the Net nominee, in 2019 his short fiction collection *North Beach and Other Stories* was awarded Finalist status in LGBTQ+ Fiction by the International Book Awards.

PW Covington is a 100% Service-Connected Disabled Veteran of the USAF, and a member of the National Writers Union (NWU).

When not traveling to support his poetry and prose, PW makes his home just south of Historic Route 66 in Albuquerque's International District, where he has worked as a stand-in or background performer for film and television productions such as *Better Call Saul*, *Duster*, and *Ransom Canyon*.

Made in the USA
Columbia, SC
17 September 2024